The Dream To Become A Butterfly

Beau D'Amico

Copyright © 2025

All Rights Reserved.

No Part of this book may be produced, stored in a retrieval system, or transmitted by any means without the written permission of the author.

ISBN: 978-0-635-44614-5

Dedication

"I dedicate this to everyone trying to find their true journey"

Author Bio

Writing to me is creating something from nothing. I love to create fun, heartfelt, inspiring stories, full of real truth, and wisdom. I began to write because meaningful stories can reshape our minds in a very magical way. Life is full of experiences, and learning lessons from those experiences make us all a better version of ourselves. I want to contribute my different perspectives, and objective knowledge to a wide audience. Everyone has a very special journey in life, and by finding our own individual purpose it makes our lives full of beauty, and wonder.

Preface

The Dream to Become a Butterfly is more than a story about a caterpillar. It's about growth, self-worth, and learning to let go of what holds us back. Maple's journey is one many of us can relate to: the desire to become something more, the pain of being misled, and the strength it takes to break free. This story touches on difficult truths, but it also offers hope. With the help of a true friend and a little courage, Maple finds the strength to become exactly what she was meant to be. I hope this story reminds anyone who reads it that change is possible, that healing is real, and that you, too, were always meant to fly.

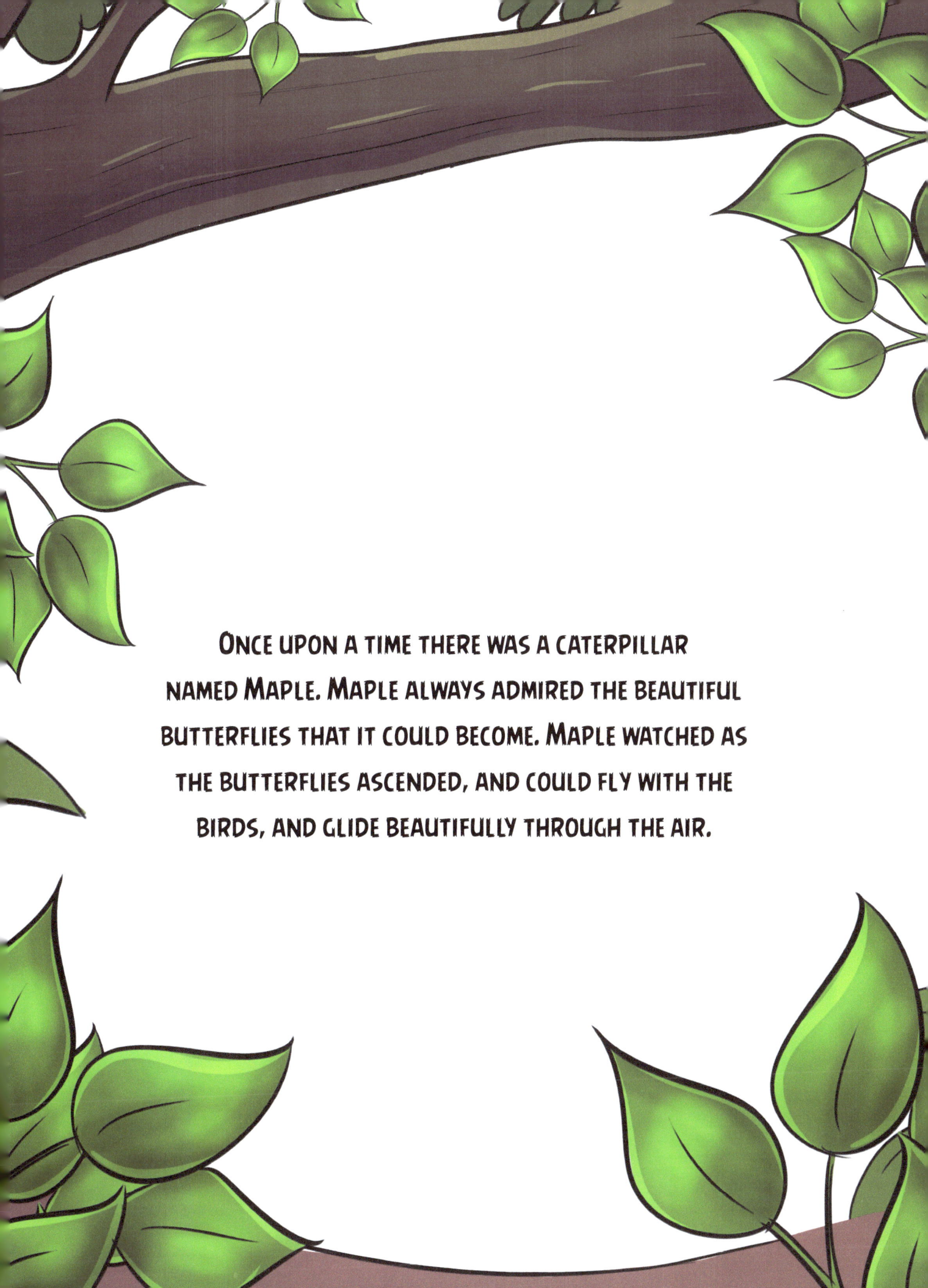

Once upon a time there was a caterpillar named Maple. Maple always admired the beautiful butterflies that it could become. Maple watched as the butterflies ascended, and could fly with the birds, and glide beautifully through the air.

One day Maple encountered a slug named Sludge. Sludge the slug also used to watch the beautiful butterflies. It angered Sludge with great envy, and resentment. Because Sludge knew it can never ascend, and become a beautiful butterfly. So Sludge came up with a sinister plan. That it would prevent Maple from becoming a butterfly. First Sludge befriended Maple, and introduced itself. Maple was so happy to make a new friend. Maple found Sludge to be very charming.

Sludge used very kind words, and complimented Maple, and its potential to become a beautiful butterfly. Sludge convinced Maple that it could help it become a butterfly quicker, and be more beautiful than the rest. Maple was so happy this new best friend knew a hidden secret. Sludge explained it could make magic slime, and by coating Maple's entire body with this essence it could make the caterpillar transform much better.

So Maple innocently agreed, and so everyday the slimy slug Sludge covered Maple's entire body with its slime. Maple felt gross, and violated every time the nasty slug Sludge did this. When Maple spoke up about how this slime made it uncomfortable. Sludge screamed at the caterpillar, and told it how ungrateful it was for receiving its magic slime. Sludge enjoyed every minute of crawling its nasty slimy body over Maple's body. Sludge even invited friends that were also slugs to also slime Maple the caterpillar's body. Maple felt confused, helpless, and that it was being ungrateful to these wonderful slugs. Especially Maple's friend the great Sludge.

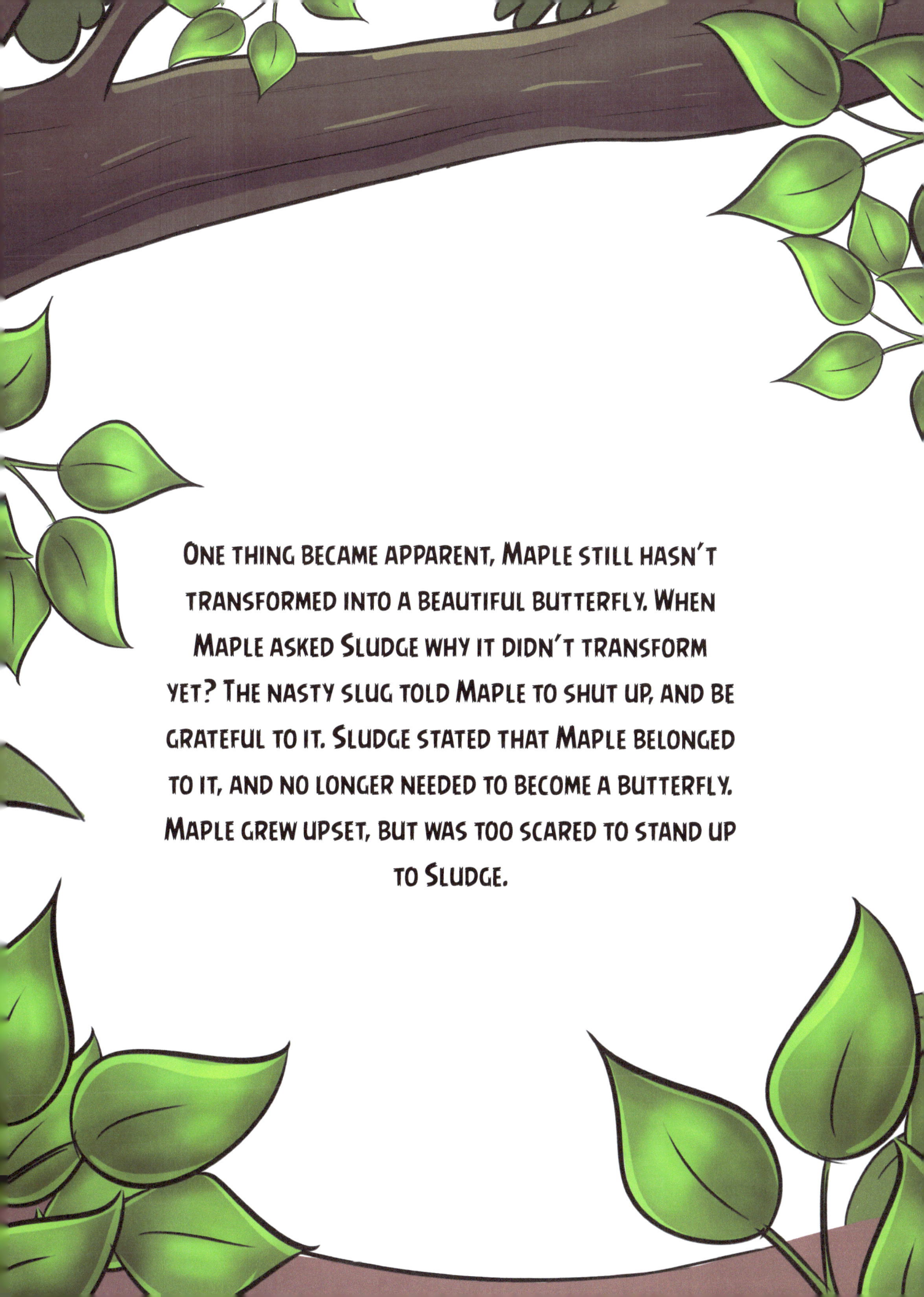

One thing became apparent, Maple still hasn't transformed into a beautiful butterfly. When Maple asked Sludge why it didn't transform yet? The nasty slug told Maple to shut up, and be grateful to it. Sludge stated that Maple belonged to it, and no longer needed to become a butterfly. Maple grew upset, but was too scared to stand up to Sludge.

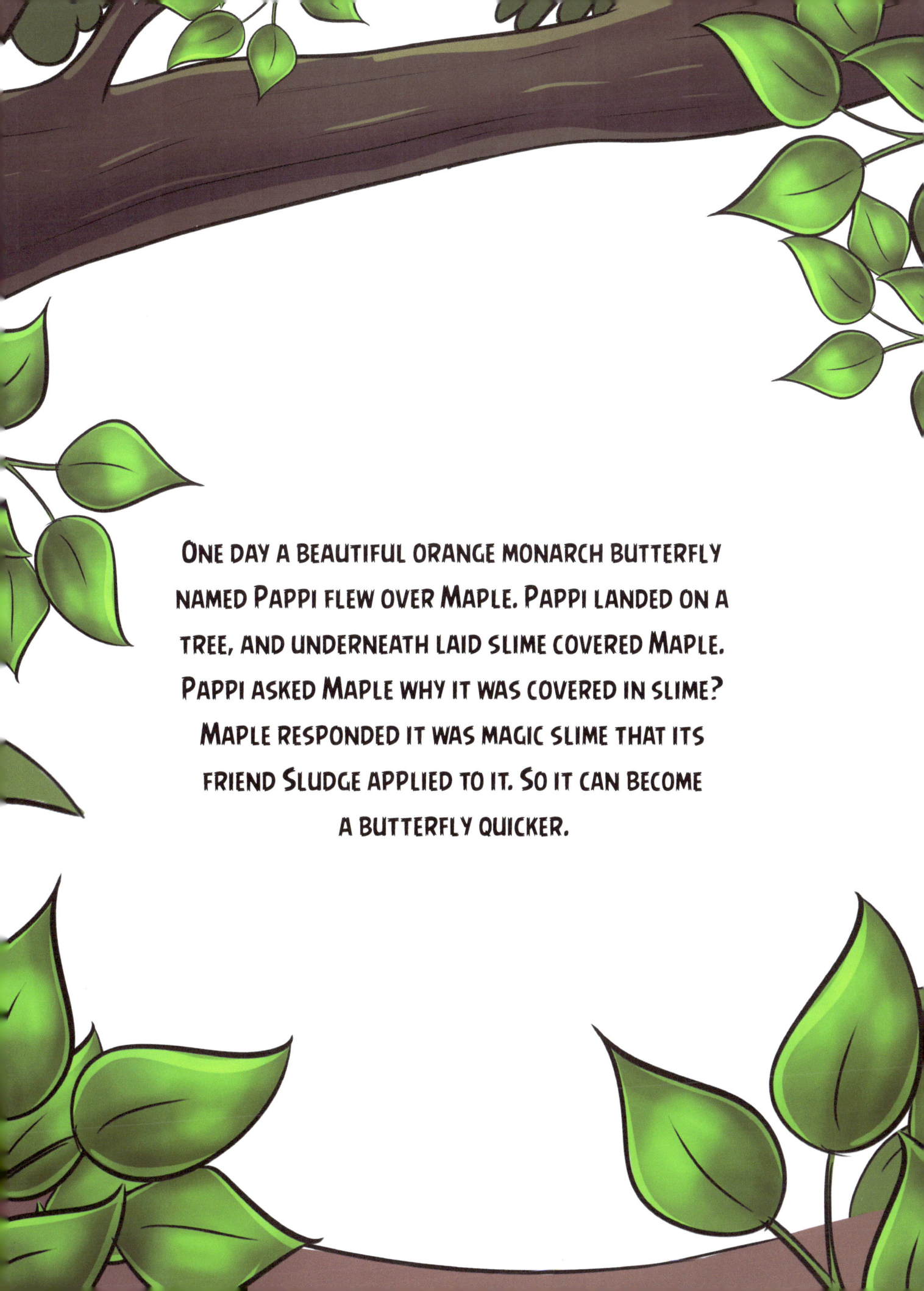

One day a beautiful orange monarch butterfly named Pappi flew over Maple. Pappi landed on a tree, and underneath laid slime covered Maple. Pappi asked Maple why it was covered in slime? Maple responded it was magic slime that its friend Sludge applied to it. So it can become a butterfly quicker.

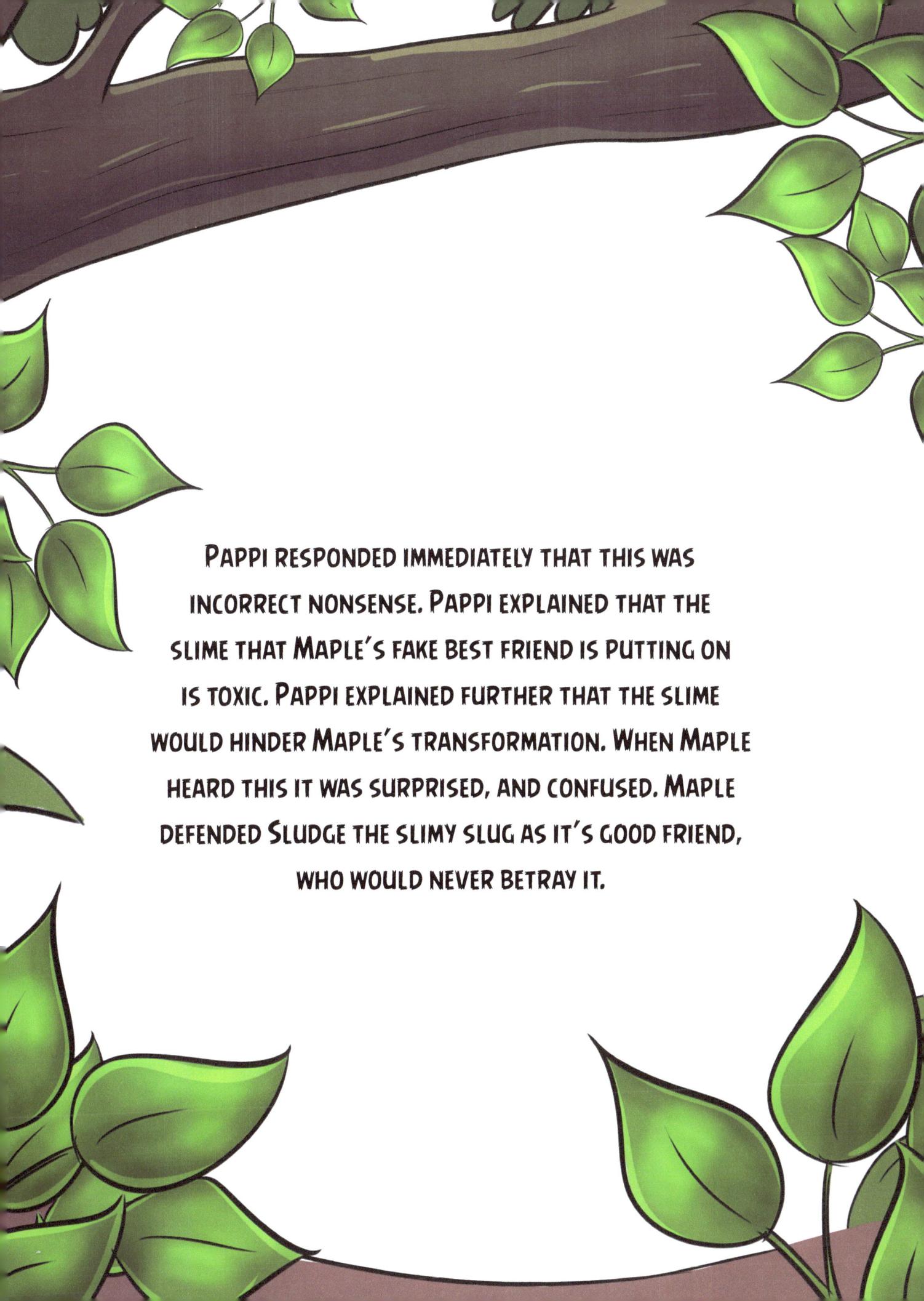

Pappi responded immediately that this was incorrect nonsense. Pappi explained that the slime that Maple's fake best friend is putting on is toxic. Pappi explained further that the slime would hinder Maple's transformation. When Maple heard this it was surprised, and confused. Maple defended Sludge the slimy slug as it's good friend, who would never betray it.

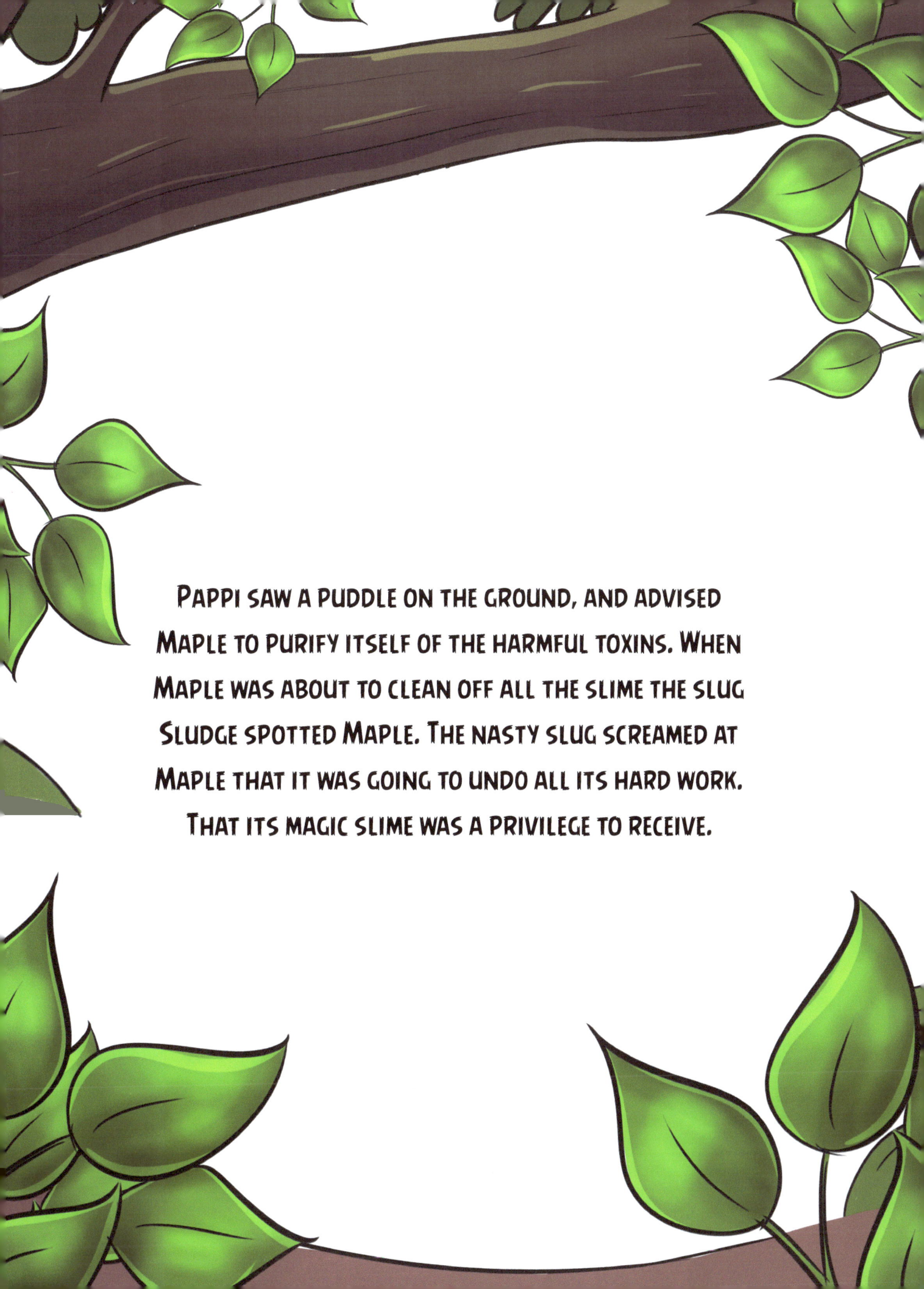

Pappi saw a puddle on the ground, and advised Maple to purify itself of the harmful toxins. When Maple was about to clean off all the slime the slug Sludge spotted Maple. The nasty slug screamed at Maple that it was going to undo all its hard work. That its magic slime was a privilege to receive.

Next Sludge started screaming at Pappi. Sludge accused Pappi of being envious that Maple would become more beautiful than itself. Pappi grew very angry at the nasty manipulative, resentful, deceitful, and envious slug. Pappi advised Maple to let it carry it away from this despicable slimy slug. Sludge approached Maple, and advised Maple to stay put. Out of fear, and uncertainty Maple froze in place.

Sludge then covered Maple with so much slime that Pappi wouldn't be able to grab it. All of a sudden it started to rain, and Sludge the slug retreated. The rain was a blessing that completely cleaned Maple of the slime.

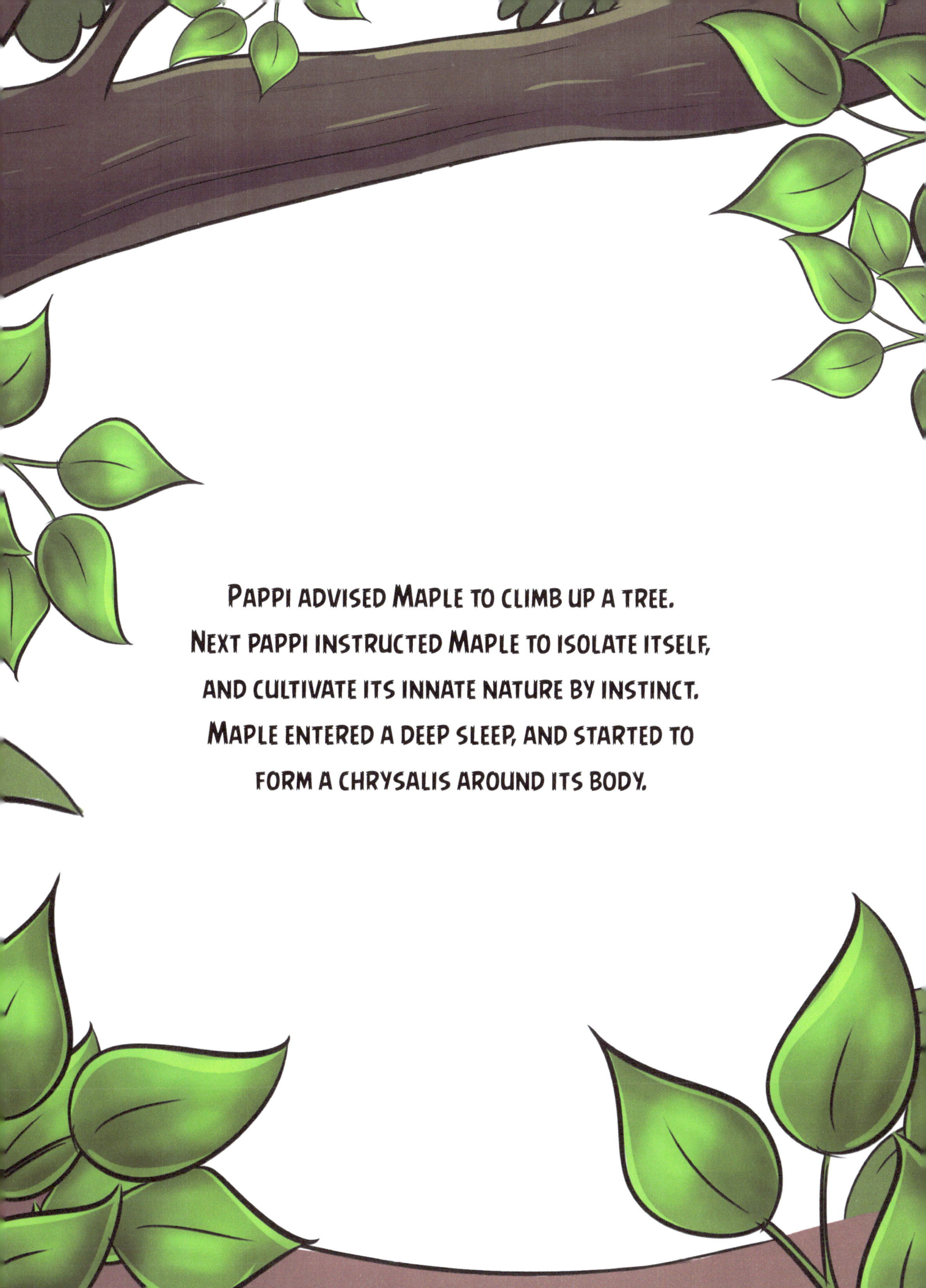

Pappi advised Maple to climb up a tree. Next pappi instructed Maple to isolate itself, and cultivate its innate nature by instinct. Maple entered a deep sleep, and started to form a chrysalis around its body.

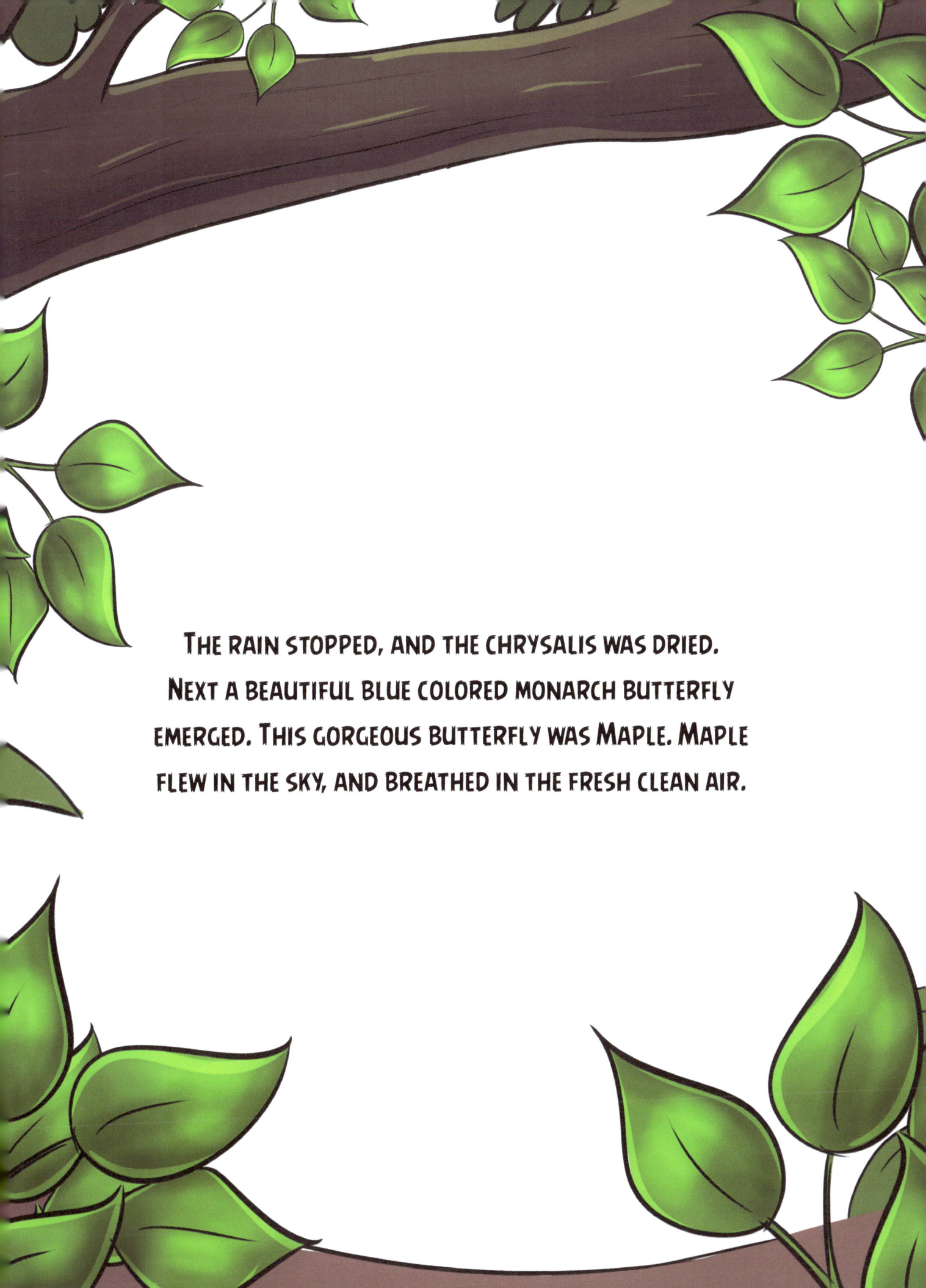

The rain stopped, and the chrysalis was dried. Next a beautiful blue colored monarch butterfly emerged. This gorgeous butterfly was Maple. Maple flew in the sky, and breathed in the fresh clean air.

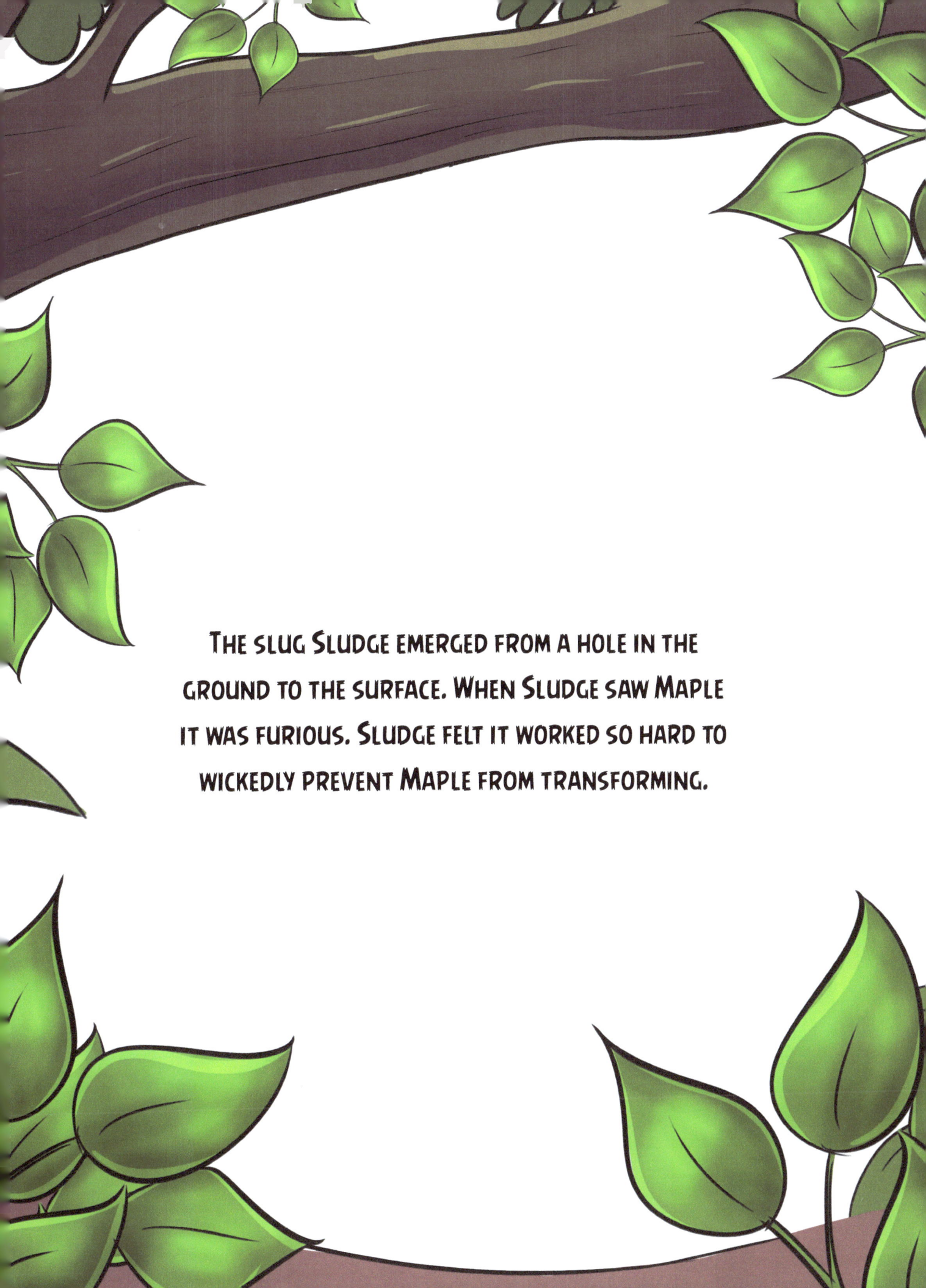

The slug Sludge emerged from a hole in the ground to the surface. When Sludge saw Maple it was furious. Sludge felt it worked so hard to wickedly prevent Maple from transforming.

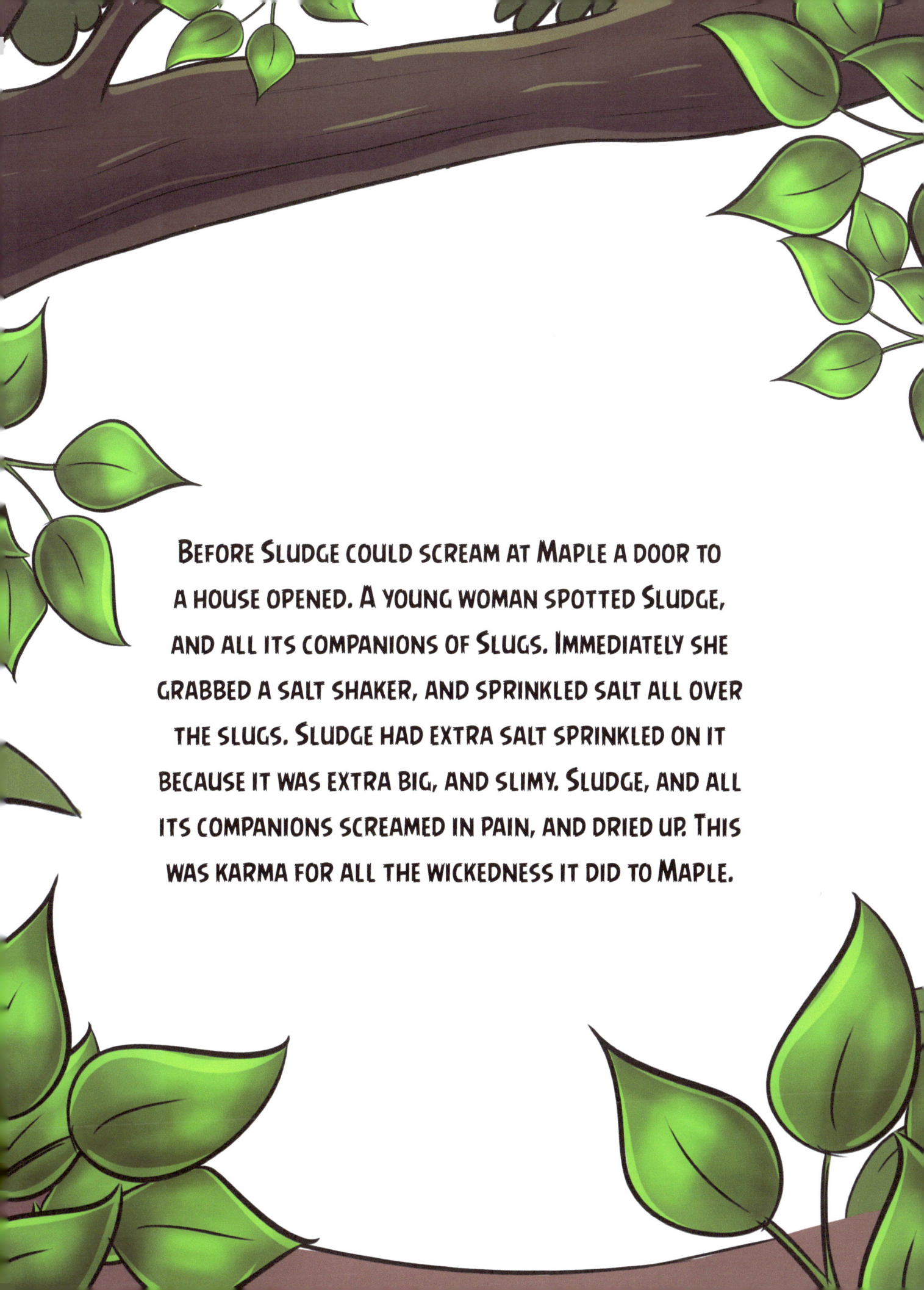

Before Sludge could scream at Maple a door to a house opened. A young woman spotted Sludge, and all its companions of Slugs. Immediately she grabbed a salt shaker, and sprinkled salt all over the slugs. Sludge had extra salt sprinkled on it because it was extra big, and slimy. Sludge, and all its companions screamed in pain, and dried up. This was karma for all the wickedness it did to Maple.

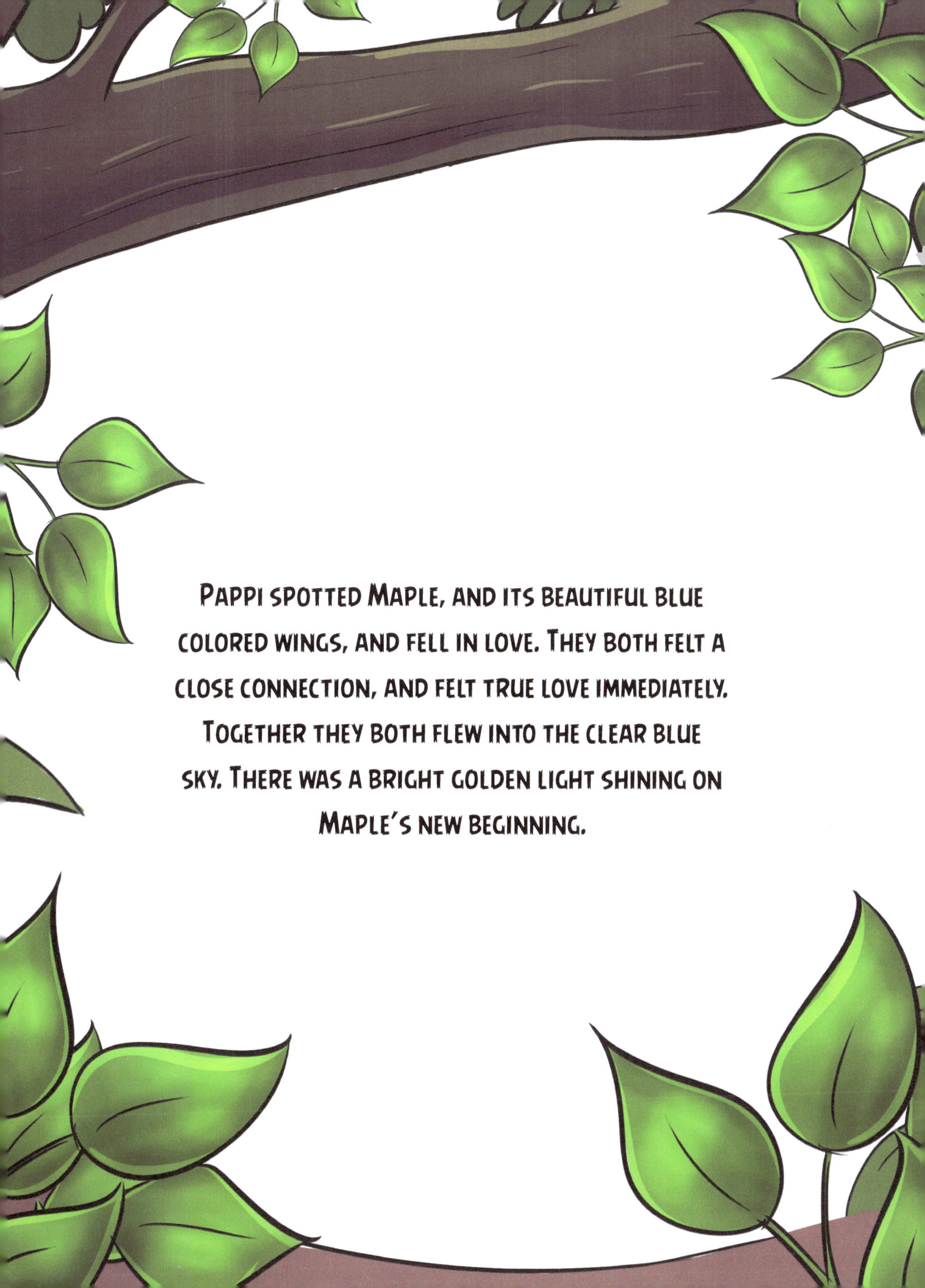

Pappi spotted Maple, and its beautiful blue colored wings, and fell in love. They both felt a close connection, and felt true love immediately. Together they both flew into the clear blue sky. There was a bright golden light shining on Maple's new beginning.

Afterword

In this story the caterpillar Maple started off naive, and ignorant to the jealous poisonous mind of Sludge. Maple became a victim to a bully that Maple mistakenly thought was a friend. It took an outsider named Pappi a monarch butterfly, to point out that it was being held back from reaching its real life purpose. The purpose being the true meaning behind Maple's existence of the transformation of becoming a butterfly. Sludge was blocking Maple with its toxic slime, and hate so Maple couldn't find its true purpose. By Maple showing self love, and going within itself it transformed into its true self becoming a beautiful butterfly. Karma occurred to sludge because negativity will always return back to where it came. The grateful ones are rewarded, and the ungrateful ones receive a harsh lesson from life's unseen justice.

Color the Magic!

Enjoyed the story?
Now it's time to bring it to life with color!

Spot the Differences

Look closely at each scene and spot five changes.

CAN YOU SPOT THE

DIFFERENCES IN SCENE 01

CAN YOU SPOT THE

FFERENCES IN SCENE 02

CAN YOU SPOT THE

DIFFERENCES IN SCENE 03

CAN YOU SPOT THE

FFERENCES IN SCENE 04

CAN YOU SPOT THE

DIFFERENCES IN SCENE 05

CAN YOU SPOT THE

FFERENCES IN SCENE 06

CAN YOU SPOT THE

DIFFERENCES IN SCENE 07

DIFFERENCES IN SCENE 08

CAN YOU SPOT THE

DIFFERENCES IN SCENE 09

CAN YOU SPOT THE

DIFFERENCES IN SCENE 10

CAN YOU SPOT THE

DIFFERENCES IN SCENE 11

CAN YOU SPOT THE

DIFFERENCES IN SCENE 12

CAN YOU SPOT THE

IFFERENCES IN SCENE 13

CAN YOU SPOT THE

DIFFERENCES IN SCENE 14

CAN YOU SPOT THE

IFFERENCES IN SCENE 15

Draw the Story Characters

Trace your favorite characters and watch them come alive.

DRAW MAPLE

DRAW PAPPI

DRAW SLUDGE

DRAW MAPLE

Word Search

Find the hidden story words waiting inside the puzzle.

WORD SEARCH NO.1

```
G C L K F P B E A U T I F U L D T H
C D D I Y W W V R T L J N O J T R P
B Z I Q P E C M Y D C I C S S O A B
U M G R T U H I N L X B H L T X N V
T R Y B R C V Q K B H J R I R I S K
T C A T E R P I L L A R Y M H C F A
E M F V E T I D D N D A S E Z Q O J
R A M F L Y T M M O T N A R J G R C
F P G K F D D S L U G P L A Y B M A
L L V O D E Y M B Y O T I I W B R X
Y E K G S L U D G E B Y S N N F S Y
S L I M Y X A K W P H T P A P P I T
```

FIND THE FOLLOWING WORDS

1. CATERPILLAR
2. BUTTERFLY
3. CHRYSALIS
4. BEAUTIFUL
5. TRANSFORM
6. SLUDGE
7. MAPLE
8. PAPPI
9. SLIME
10. TOXIC
11. SLIMY
12. SLUG
13. RAIN
14. TREE
15. FLY

WORD SEARCH NO. 2

C	R	A	W	L	E	N	O	M	G	X	Z	H	K	M	X	M	W
L	K	P	R	O	T	E	C	T	O	H	S	E	G	F	N	I	C
F	S	P	L	I	G	H	T	F	L	Z	A	L	H	Q	S	W	A
P	Y	Q	P	U	X	L	J	D	D	U	L	P	Y	F	N	O	F
J	U	L	E	U	Y	O	F	U	E	T	T	L	A	S	Q	M	B
S	L	R	N	Y	D	Y	B	U	N	O	L	E	P	C	S	A	S
K	O	Y	I	W	B	D	L	G	R	V	J	S	I	X	C	N	Y
Y	P	O	X	F	I	L	L	X	B	I	R	S	J	F	R	T	V
U	R	V	A	I	Y	N	Q	E	L	L	O	B	X	F	E	S	V
C	O	Q	C	Z	N	R	G	I	U	E	C	U	V	O	A	W	Z
W	K	D	C	R	B	V	M	S	E	W	B	K	S	Q	M	W	K
Y	A	C	H	I	N	N	O	C	E	N	T	H	K	T	M	I	S

FIND THE FOLLOWING WORDS

1. HELPLESS
2. INNOCENT
3. FURIOUS
4. PROTECT
5. PUDDLE
6. GOLDEN
7. SCREAM
8. PURIFY
9. WOMAN
10. WINGS
11. LIGHT
12. CRAWL
13. SALT
14. BLUE
15. SKY

Maze Adventure

Help the characters find their way through the winding paths.

MAZE NO.1

HELP MAPLE TRANSFORM INTO A BUTTERFLY

MAZE NO.2

HELP PAPPI REACH MAPLE

MAZE NO.3

HELP SLUDGE REACH HIS FRIENDS

See You Next Time!

Thank you for joining me on this adventure. I hope you enjoyed the story, had fun with the activities, and discovered something new along the way. I wrote this story to make reading exciting and meaningful, with a little magic and a little lesson on every page. Bye for now, and see you in the next adventure.

Beau D'Amico